H U É

Photography by Thomas Renaut
Text and captions by Michel Hoàng
Drawings by Jean-Christophe Marchal & François Greck
English translation by Josephine Bacon

Publication assisted by a grant from the Regional Council of Nord-Pas de Calais

RÉGION
NORD
PAS DE CALAIS

CONSEIL RÉGIONAL

Les Éditions d'Indochine

CONTENTS

6

A PRESTIGIOUS HERITAGE

Hué is a gift to Vietnam from Champa. To explain this one must go back in history. In the third century B.C., the Chinese of the Han Dynasty built a command post and fortress at Hué. Later, in the third century A.D., on the probable site of the arenas, a Cham city was founded, which bore the name of Kandarpupura. It is in this region of Indo-China that the rift opened up between the Chinese civilisation in the north and that of Indian culture in the south. During the first five centuries of the Christian era, Chinese peoples from southern Asia and peoples from the islands of the Pacific who were of Indian origin settled around the Gate of Annam (at about the 18th parallel). The latter group, who were later joined by Indonesian peoples of uncertain origin, became the Cham people, founders of the Champa kingdom. The Cham were influenced by China in material things but were under the spiritual influence of India. At first they fought the Chinese but later created maritime principalities which traded with other Indianised kingdoms such as Java. From the fifth to the tenth centuries, the Champa attained their zenith, rivalling the Khmer empire, thanks to the Chinese lack of interest in the Indo-chinese peninsula. The evidence lies in the capital cities (Sinhapura, Indrapura, Vijaya) and the impressive religious centres (Po Nagar, Srisanabhadresvara - in Vietnamese, Thap Bà and Mi-son). The Viêt peoples - the future Vietnamese - whose centre of gravity is the Red River delta, emancipated themselves from 1,000 years of Chinese domination and, from the time of the Dai-Viêt kingdom (939) gradually conquered the coasts of the peninsula to the detriment of the Cham. In 1306, after numerous battles, the Cham king, Jaya Simhavarman III, handed over two districts, in exchange for the hand of a Viet princess. These included Kandar-pupura (Hué). Despite further conflicts which caused it to change hands yet again, Hué, the gift of the Cham, would

Ceremony of the elephants in front of the Comat, inside the citadel (left-hand page). Portrait of the emperor Dui-Tan (centre). Court musicians by the Midday Gate (left).

Life at court was eventful for the diplomats. A reception for a French delegation at the Palace (left-hand page) and the Ambassadors' District in 1884 (above).
Facing, the Gia Long court returns to Hué from Qui-Nhon, the residence of the French governor (1902).

Pre-war scenes are particularly informative since they show how the imperial city was actually run. The Palace and the French-style gardens are visible (facing above and right); they have now gone.

This aerial view shows the Vauban-style structure of the Citadel (opposite, below).

remain henceforth in Vietnam. More territories were lost by the Cham and in 1471, the capital of Champa, Vijaya, fell to the Dai-Viêt. The last Cham king was killed in 1692; Champa became a vassal. In 1822, the purely nominal power of the last Cham princes was abolished and Champa disappeared.

All that remains today are a few hundred thousand Cham, assimilated and acculturated, yet central Vietnam still bears their cultural imprint. For instance, a lot of place names, even those which have been Vietnamised, still indicate their Cham past. Place names such as Chiêm-thành or Dai-Chiêm Hai-khau retain the term 'Chiêm' - Cham, in Vietnamese. Wherever there were hermitages, temples to Shiva, the Vietnamese have often kept the religious connotation of the place, as in Rùng Dàng (Sacred forest), Côn Dàng (sacred hill). Around and to the south of Hué, traces of the Cham can be found in the geography and folklore. These people, the Etruscans of Vietnam, had a civilisation which preceded that of the Vietnamese by a thousand years, but which the Vietnamese ultimately swept away.

THE NEW CAPITAL

From the moment when, weakened and beaten, the Champa were reduced to a shadow of their former selves, the Vietnamese began to write their own history on the conquered lands. After 1427, the Lê royal family was destabilised by a prolonged civil war between the feudal clans of Trinh, Mac and Nguyên, who all tried to seize power. In 1637, the nobleman Nguyên Hoàng founded a new citadel on the site of Hué. According to a famous Vietnamese legend, a "Celestial Woman", dressed in red and green, appeared to Nguyên Hoàng, in 1601, to toll him that whoever built a city at this spot would reign for many years. From that moment, Phu Xuân (the future Hué) became the capital of the Nguyêns, who installed themselves in central Vietnam, while waging war simultaneously against the Cham, the Khmers and the Trinh clan.

In 1771, a peasants' revolt broke out, uniting the poor peasants, the Cham, the ethnic minorities and the Chinese merchants against the Nguyên. It was called the Tây-Son Rebellion, and was led by three brothers who narrowly missed toppling the Nguyêns by occupying Phu Xuân. The young prince Nguyên Anh narrowly escaped the massacres and called upon Siam and France for assistance. He obtained the support of Monseigneur Pigneau de Béhaine who hired French mercenaries to save the prince, whom he hoped to make his protégé and the instrument of his missionary plans. In 1802 Nguyên Anh again took up residence in Phu Xuân and had himself crowned there under the name Gia Long. His capital was renamed Hué (a distortion of Hoa, 'harmony') and his country, unified from north to south, became the empire of Dai-Nam (Great South), replacing the name An-Nam (Pacified South) which it had been given by China.

Life in Hué was full of pomp and ceremony. These examples show a wedding parade through the streets of the city (opposite) and a photo of the municipal brass band in 1936 (below).

Thanks to its position between the mountains which could serve as a refuge, and the sea, which promoted sea trading, Hué supplanted Thang Long (Hà Nôi) as the capital. A French officer, de Puymanel, planned for Hué to be protected by a fortified wall in the Vauban style, once dykes had been built along the riverside to prevent autumnal flooding. In 1818, ramparts were built, in which there were four gates. The fortifications included bastions, corner lookouts, curtain walls, scarps

Ministers of the Court (below opposite) and mandarins arriving at a reception in 1952 (facing, above). The imperial retinue leaving the citadel for the Hill of the Heavens during the ceremony of Nam Giao in 1956 (right-hand page, above). Emperor Bao Dai descends from the sedan chair, a gift from Louis XVI (right-hand page, centre). The funeral cortege at the tomb of Dong Kanh pays its last respects (right).

and parapets. Yet the moats and walls did not protect the Citadel from the heavy flooding of 1820, 1822, 1844 and 1904.

As described by Europeans in the 18th century (Fathers Koffler and Vachet), the capital was modelled on Peking under the Ming Dynasty (1368-1644). It consisted of three separate cities which were enclosed within each other, the capital city (Kinh-Thành), the imperial city (Hoàng-Thành) and the Forbidden Purple City (Tu-Câm-Thành). This architectural whole was constructed on the principles of Chinese geomancy set within a landscape which 'generated' the city because it was the emanation thereof. Hué is thus protected by a ring of natural, symbolic, sacred sites which are supposed to be propitious and are sometimes secret. The first lies one mile outside the city, on the same bank of the river, and is the mound on which stands the Pagoda of the Celestial Woman (Thiên-Mu). Standing as it does beside the capital and built on the remains of a Cham temple, it is known as the 'Magic Mountain' sheltering the two protectors of the Earth. About a mile to the south, the Hill of the Southern District (Nam Giao) is also called Hill of the Heavenly Sacrifice and is an imitation of the Temple of the Heavens in Peking. The first rectangular walkway of the four superimposed terraces symbolises the underworld, the next two are square and symbolise the Earth, and the last, which is rounded, the Sky. The Hill of Ngu-binh (called the Screen of the King) consists of five concentric terraces, to protect the Palace against ill winds.

THE SILENT CITADEL

eat of the imperial throne and of the government, Hué was home to the rulers of the day. The capitol (or Citadel) was the domain of the mandarins, who in theory came from the people because they gained their posts through competitive examinations which were open to anyone who could pass them. Inside the Citadel was the Censor's Office and the Council of Sages, the supreme body of imperial authority based on Confucian principles, the Imperial Academy, responsible for drafting laws and finally the College of the Sons of State, a sort of School of Administration.

The vermillion and gilt wood-panelled Hall of Supreme Harmony - the throne room.- measures 1400 square metres. (left hand page and drawing). Reception rooms are also finely decorated (top photo).

The imperial city was home to the royal family and the seat of government. It also housed the Dynastic Council which was responsible for investigating the imperial genealogy and ritual and the Higher Institute of Medicine at which the Court physicians officiated.

At the very heart of the Forbidden Purple City (so-called because of the colour of its walls and because it was forbidden to commoners) lived the monarch, his imperial household and the eunuchs.

The mandarins of the high echelon were summoned here and ordered to issue edicts and decree covering the six most important ministries (Interior, Treasury, Justice, Rites, Army and Public

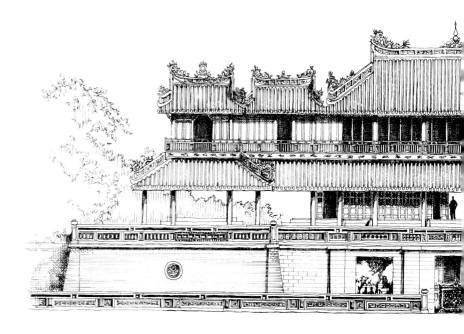

Views of the Imperial City can be glimpsed through elegant gong-shaped or fan-shaped openings (opposite). This dragon, the symbol of imperial power, winds around a bronze column. The south door, enlarged in the early 19th century, constitutes the main entrance to the Imperial City. (previous page and above)

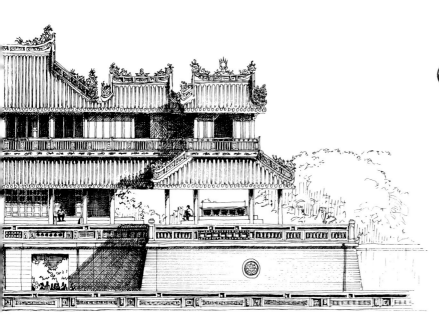

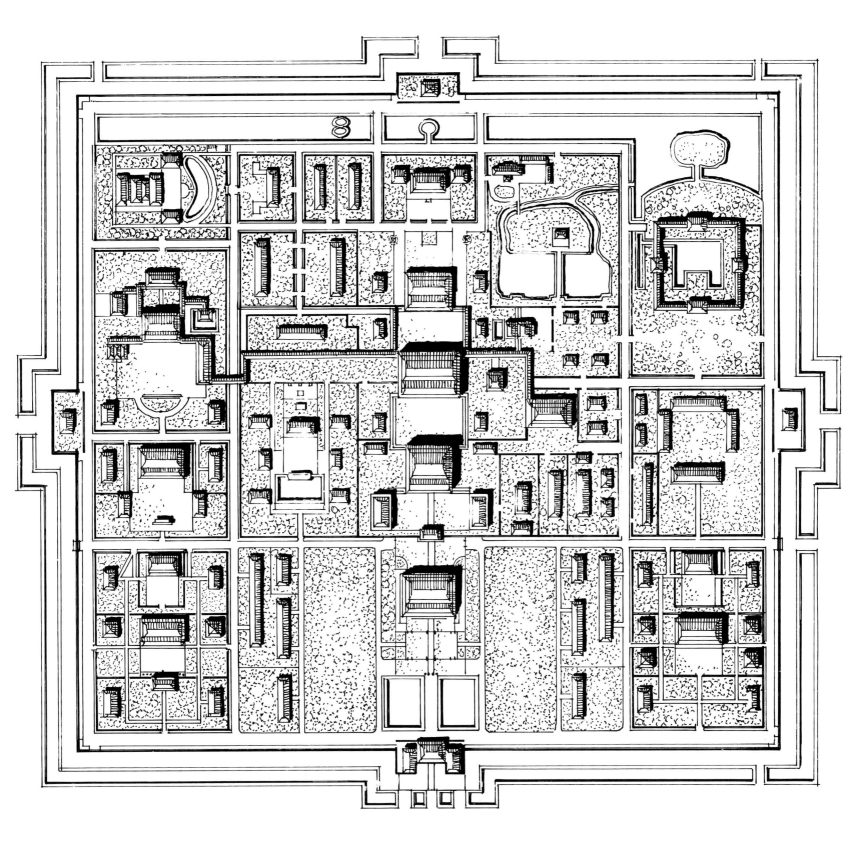

Works). The Great Secretariat, acting as a chancellery also met here as did the High Court of Justice, a court of appeal. Finally, the Secret Council (Co Mât) also met here. It discussed the most important affairs of state and its members were all appointed by the king.

Designed on the traditional Chinese pattern, the Citadel was bisected by a symbolic north-south road. The eastern half (older, superior, masculine and civil) housed the cultural activities – a library, gardens, a theatre and the civil mandarinate. The western half (younger, inferior, feminine and military) contained the houses of the princesses and concubines and

One of the four great bronze cauldrons in archaic Chinese style.(above).
An ancient canon is poised on its carriage, awaiting an unlikely enemy. Between 1803 and 1804 the emperor Gia Long melted down the Nine Cannons (Cuu Vi), the guardians of the Empire. Dedicated to the four seasons and the five elements, they regularly received ritual offerings (right).
The plan of the Imperial City (opposite).
Few of these buildings are still standing..

the military mandarinate.

Within the Purple City, the South revealed the public persona of the sovereign – reception rooms and public services, while the North contained all that was connected with his private life, his residence and that of the Empress, and pavilions for reading and meditation.

At each corner of the Imperial City there stood the ancestral temples of the Nguyên: Trieû Miêu dedicated to Nguyên Kim and his consort, a royal couple of the ancient dynasty; Thai Miêu, dedicated to the nine lords who ruled prior to the emperor, Gia Long; a third was devoted to the secondary cult of the servants of the dynasty, but this, together with the fourth temple, has now been destroyed.

THE CULTURAL TRADITION

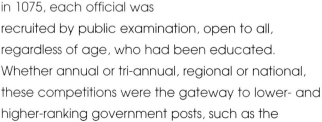

Hué was also the nursery of the mandarinate, that administrative and political system inherited from China and based on a 'meritocracy'. Starting in 1075, each official was recruited by public examination, open to all, regardless of age, who had been educated. Whether annual or tri-annual, regional or national, these competitions were the gateway to lower- and higher-ranking government posts, such as the

23

governor of a province. Those who passed received the degrees of bachelor (*tu tài*), master (*cu nhân*) and the most prestigious title of doctor (*tien si*). The examination hall was the 'camp of the lettered', within the Citadel. Here, equipped only with the bare necessities and closely supervised, the candidates laboured for days at a time, because some stages lasted for 12 hours. The extreme difficulty of the competition meant that few were able to pass. There were only 2,000 candidates who passed the doctoral degree between 1075 and 1918, when the last examinations for the mandarinate were held. The examinations all included literary dissertations and compositions in verse, though some required a knowledge of administration or law. The Chinese classics were a compulsory subject and the language used was literary Chinese which, like Latin in medieval Europe, was the language of scholarship. These tests were not so much a preparation for a career as a tax inspector, overseer or administrator but rather for the 'art of governance', enshrined in the maxim *thuân thiên ung dân* (follow the Heavens to respond to the people). This is no doubt the reason for the obsolescence of a system, which may have been

An imposing portico of very dilapidated stucco-covered brick leads to the Pavilion of Splendour, the Hiên Lâm Cac (main photograph). The gate is hidden behind a wooden partition decorated with stylised Chinese characters (Photo above) whilst one can see the The pavilion from the windows (lower photograph).

The upper drawing on the right shows a detail of one of the nine dynastic urns, symbols of the immutability of the Vietnamese Empire. These bronze vases, which weigh almost two tons, face the dynastic temple of Thê Miêu, opposite the imperial altars (lower drawing).

Facing is an interior door of Hiêm Lâm Cac whose elaborate carvings are highlighted by the old gold paintwork.

龍

27

*This pavilion houses the votive altars
of the 15 emperors who reigned from Hué.
One of them is adorned with the portrait of Duy Tan as a child
(crowned at the age of eight). He rebelled against France in 1916 and
was exiled, but trained as an engineer and joined the French resistance
led by de Gaulle. He was killed in a plane crash in 1945.
(Right-hand photo).
These Asiatic halbards and lances were used as ritual armaments
for ceremonial purposes (below).*

tried and tested for centuries, but needed to be reformed and modernised. Nevertheless, it was taken over and used, in a less powerful form by the colonial administration.

The cultural tradition centred around Hué still persisted. After the Imperial Academy, the Quôc Hoc Lycée produced generations of intellectuals, including Hô Chi Minh and his colleagues, Pham Van Dông and Vo Nguyên Giap, historian and conqueror of Diên Biên Phu. There are many literary giants who emerged from Hué, such as the poet, Nguyên Dinh Chiêu, the revolutionary and writer, Phan Bôi Châu and many more. Today in Hué, the French literary tradition has survived, and many of its intellectuals can expound in impeccable French on the works of André Gide or Marguerite Duras.

END OF THE REIGN

Thirteen emperors ruled from Hué. The last of the Nguyên dynasty met a sad fate, subservient to a colonial power and ruined by war. In 1883 the French, competing with the British for Chinese trade, captured Hué. Julien Viaud, a naval officer who took part in the siege sent a report of the action to the Paris newspaper, *Le Figaro*. It realistically described the killings and the sacking of the city by French soldiers and caused a scandal in Paris when news of the massacres behind the colonial 'gesture' reached Paris. The author of the article was naturally summoned by the Admiralty, to explain himself. He

had used the pseudonym Pierre Loti.

As the French presence grew ever more authoritarian, the prerogatives of the Court of Hué were gradually reduced to nothing. The local power hesitated, attempting to manoeuvre and negotiate with the occupier. Collaborationist parties were formed, but others chose the path of resistance.

From 1883, the fate of the emperors of Hué was sealed, their court in crisis. Tu Duc, deposed and incarcerated, died of starvation in 1883. In the same year, his successor, Hiêp Hoa, died in suspicious circumstances, poisoned or asphyxiated by a concubine. Khien Phuc, who died in 1884, was probably strangled. Ham Nghi took part in an anti-French insurrection and was exiled to Algeria in 1888. Isolated and bitter, Dong Khanh died of malaria in 1889. Than Thai was deposed for alleged insanity, then exiled

This succession of moss-encrusted gateways covers the passageway to the queen-mother's pavilion. Every morning, the emperor would use this route to make a formal visit to his mother. A window in the Luong Phung, pavilion in the queen-mother's residence shows the wealth of detailed decoration in even the most insignificant ornament (right).

to Algeria. Duy Tan fomented a rebellion which failed and was in turn exiled to the island of Reunion in 1916. In 1940, he sided with General de Gaulle but was killed in 1945 in an aeroplane accident. Khai Dinh tried in vain to cast off the French yoke. Upon his death, in 1925, he was succeeded by Bao Dai, a mere figurehead, lacking prestige and popularity.This frivolous monarch, who was both manipulator and manipulated, abdicated in 1945. In 1955, he sought asylum in France.

This series of unhappy reigns illustrates the vicissitudes of the Court of Hué, gripped by internecine strife caused by feeble, powerless emperors. In this climate of imperial decline, threatened from outside and required to make radical reforms, the Court was unable to cope with this turning-point in history. Subsequent reforms were met with radical repression resulting in rebellion.

The deserted courtyards of the dilapidated palaces, worm-eaten wooden columns and overgrown gardens are a far cry from the city which W. Somerset Maugham, writing in 1930, described as having "something of the leisurely air of a cathedral city in the West of England".

*A wall pierced with a design of frogs
surrounding the Chinese symbol for longevity
contrasts with the floral decoration of another
pierced opening (above).
Multicoloured ceramic mandarins decorate
the frontage of the recently renovated theatre,
in which the court was entertained with
classical plays known as 'tuong'
(above, centre and below right).
An elaborate wooden construction of the type
for which local craftsmen are famous is
illustrated on the left.*

These boys returning from a fishing trip are shown against the East Gate of the Citadel, looking like something out of their history books (left). The North Gate (above right) and the East Gate (above left) are less elaborately carved.

THE VALLEY OF THE TOMBS

 trangely, these emperors who were greater poets than they were rulers, have found exaltation in death. Their tombs, rather than their reigns, have magnified them and opened the gates of posterity to them.

The cult of ancestor worship continues in modern Vietnam because it protects the living. For this reason, death takes on a metaphysical, philosophical nature, since it is an integral part of existence. According to buddhist beliefs, the soul transmigrates into a world beyond the senses. To ensure the survival of the soul the human body must be preserved intact and any damage to it is to be avoided.

An artificial lake covered with aquatic vegetation in the garden of an ancient pavilion is the unlikely setting for the necropolis of the emperor Tu Duc. (Main photo) Facing, entrance to the mausoleum of the emperor-poet who was also an authoritarian ruler.

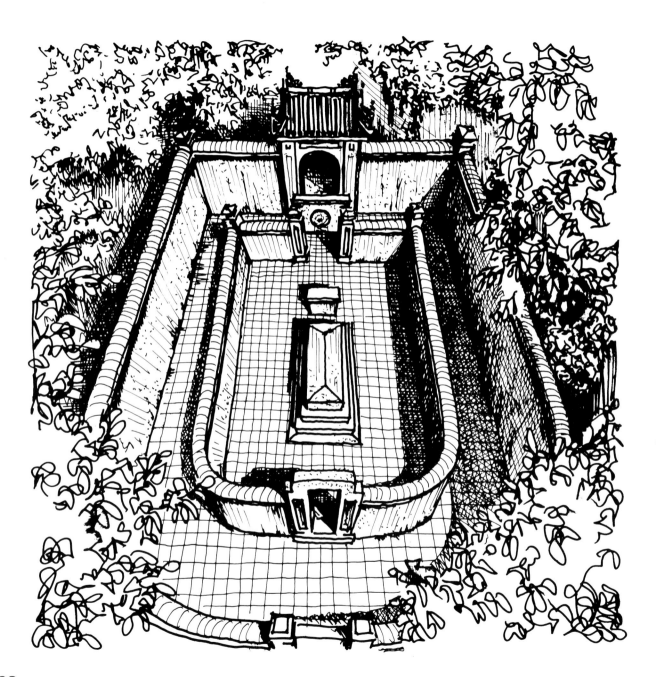

The tomb of Tu Duc and the funeral stele of the monarch , (right) adorned with Chinese ideograms extolling his virtues. Left, an unusual view of the tomb of the wife of Tu Duc, protected by a two surrounding walls.

The religious rites and observances of the Hué Imperial court were inextricably linked to the exercise of power. That is why the imperial tombs, modelled on those of the Ming dynasty in China, were erected in a sort of 'valley of the dead', which was an integral part of the capital, and were protected both physically and symbolically. The tombs, which were often erected during the monarch's lifetime, consist of a group of buildings set in landscaped gardens. Architecture and nature complement each other here, since man and nature must be balanced.

Tree-covered hillocks,

Left, several views of the mausoleum of Minh Mang:
The statue of the mandarin stands on eternal guard in the
courtyard of the deceased emperor (top right).
The ritual vase is in the style of the Shang dynasty of China
(above).

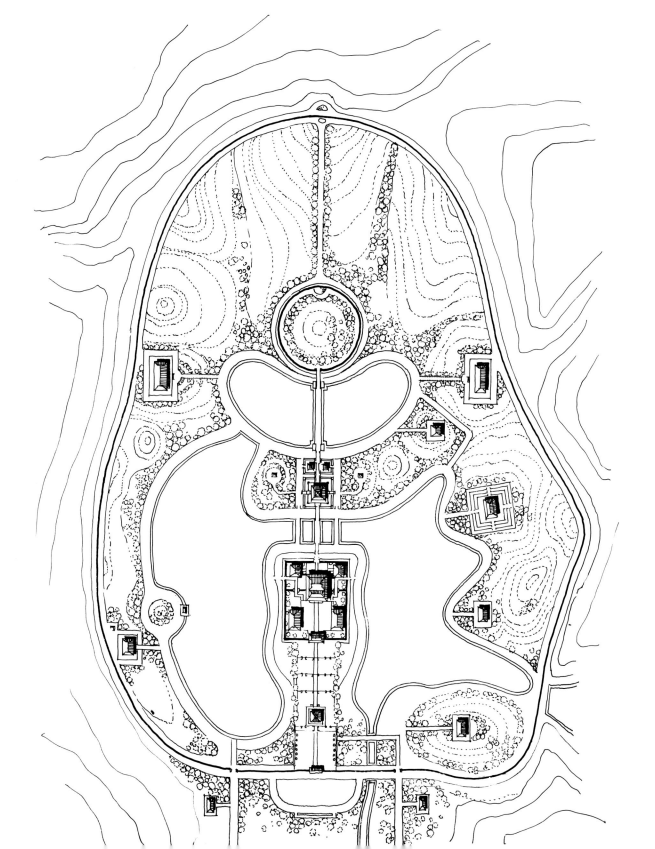

41

When the sun sets on the valley of the tombs, the Perfumed River becomes a blue-grey mirror of steel, reflecting the remains of the day *(preceding pages)*.
Inside the mausoleum of Minh Mang. The Chinese character *(left-hand page)* represents virtue. A small brazier holding joss-sticks stands on a votive table *(right)* and a potted fern provides a touch of green *(below)*.

45

deep, lotus-filled ponds and shaded, fragrant footpaths constitute the landscape in which the sepulchres are set. This looks nothing like a mausoleum in the West, however grandiose. Greenery is everywhere here, and the senses are charmed by the scent of rare perfumes, the tinkling of fountains and the smoothness of mineral shapes. This place of eternal rest is a hymn to life. As in China, the tombs of Hué consist of three parts. First there is the tomb, then the temple of the soul of the deceased with precious objects which belonged to him and which are designed to be used by him in the Beyond. This is where the veil which held the monarch's last breath is kept and here, too, is the funerary shelf on which sacrifices are placed from time to time.

Then there is a

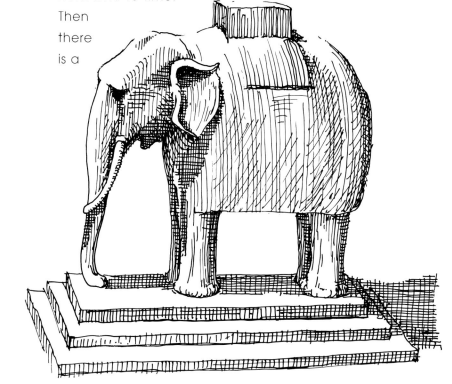

The peaceful atmosphere of the necropolis of the Nguyên dynasty is an invitation to
meditation upon the sweetness and pain of an existence which is all too fleeting.
Translucent ceramics and chinese characters are arranged along the length of the
double row of tiles on the roof of a pavilion topped by shining dragons, a gem of
funerary architecture (above).

massive, imposing stele on which the official virtues of the sovereign are inscribed in Chinese ideograms. There may also be an adjoining terrace for ceremonies.

The tombs, which are not of equal importance, were built to receive the remains of the 13 Nguyên emperors. That of Gia Long (1802-1819) and his immediate heirs, Minh Mang (1820-1840), Thieu Tri (1841-1847) and Tu Duc (1847-1883) are the most magnificent, elegant and traditional.

Gia Long's tomb stands alone on a picturesque hill. Despite the ravages of time, the mausoleum, surrounded by a six-level terrace, retains an eternal charm.

More monumental and sumptuous, the tomb of Minh Mang, with the Palace of Light reflected in a crescent-shaped lake is undeniably beautiful. It recalls the words of the poet, Minh Mang: 'This delightful countryside plunges me, from morning to night, into meditation on the art of ruling and governing'.

Tu Duc, himself a poet, has a necropolis whose concourse is decorated with statues of people and animals.The sovereign enjoyed coming here to fish or write verses in the pleasure pavilion reflected in the lake. According to tradition, the grave-diggers - who came from the ethnic minorities - were executed after performing their task, in order to keep secret the actual

The bucolic landscape (below) which leads to the tomb of the emperor Gia Long and his wife. The tomb is surrounded by a double wal (right).

50

whereabouts of
the tomb.

Writing about
the more modern
tomb of Dong
Khanh (1885-
1889), Roland
Dorgelès advised:
'But above all, do not
follow the ill-favoured guide who would lead you
to the tomb of Dong Khanh... If you visit it, the
spell will be broken'. What would he have said
about the tomb of Khai Dinh, a riot of roccoco in
which vanity and self-satisfaction replaced
artistry and craftsmanship? The last emperor, Bao
Dai, is the only one who has no tomb. That is
because he died in exile, having been
banished to France.

Red and gold vertical inscriptions, halbards and ceremonial canopies are a permanent reminder of
imperial grandeur and the imperial livery in this pagoda near Hué (left-hand page).
In the Thiên Mu Pagoda, a stele rests on the back of a giant tortoise, a symbol of longevity. A fierce-
looking moustachioed figure stands guard at the sanctuary of Thiên Mu (above).

Rows of mandarins in civilian and military
dress form a guard of honour on the concourse
of the tomb of Khai Dinh, father of Bao Dai
(above left).
This tomb was built as recently as 1928,
and stands on a hill with a panoramic view
(centre and facing drawing).
Inside, the decoration is reminiscent of that
of over-decorated European palaces (below).
Khai Dinh's statue is life size. This
imperial tomb looks unlike the others in the
Valley of the Dead (following pages)

A Living City

ar away from the pagodas and pavilions and the moss-covered city walls, lies modern Hué, a city with a population of 300,000 continues it rather languid existence. This city was subjected to bombing, there was a terrible fire in1947 and it was the scene of some of the worst fighting in the Vietnam War in 1968, when the Viêt-Công, who had managed to dislodge the South Vietnamese and American troops from the citadel, held it for one month. During the War, Trinh Công Son, a singer idolised by Vietnamese youth, sang of the horrors of civil war. His songs were condemned by the governments of both Saigon and Hanoi which described them as 'yellow' (traitorous) music, but they were hummed and played by both sides. Peace was restored a generation ago, but Hué does not seem to be part of the

economic boom currently being experienced by Vietnam as a whole. Unlike Hô Chi Minh City (Saigon), Vung Tau or Hanoi it has seen little foreign investment. Yet Hué could become a pivot in a North-South development corridor. The development of the central region is a condition for national cohesion. In 1996, Hué was declared a provincial city and now has its own development plan.

On the lawns of the ramparts, schoolchildren are playing chess (left). A permanently lacquered smile in a little booth in the town centre (opposite). A young craftsman carefully restores the panels of the South Door. UNESCO is restoring Hué's monuments, repairing the ravages of the years and of the War (above, right).

The more affluent youth indulge in *'mai diên tu'* (computer games) and Dream III Honda motorbikes. They spend their time in the *'cà-phê''* listening to disco music and the songs of local pop star Nha Phuong. There are 70,000 young people of school and student age in Hué and their greatest fear is unemployment.

Water is a vital element in Hué. It is the source of life, a means of communication, and a place of contemplation; the river and canals are an essential part of everyday life. While buffalo wallow in the muddy shallows, waterweed is collected from the river bed (below right).

In the early morning, traders unload their yoked baskets of fruit and vegetables and hurry off to their market stalls (above right).

At dusk, beside the monument to the fallen, a fragment of a poem by Nguyên Binh Kiêm (1491-1585) comes to mind:
"Thuyên co gio, mac con phiêu..": 'the boat drifts, propelled by the wind ..." (left-hand photograph).*

59

Scenes from daily life:
In the early morning, young and old practise tai
chi chuan and or 'qigong', exercises for controling
energy and breathing (above right). A rickshaw
driver carries his mid-morning snack with him
(centre). Dozens of varieties of rice are heaped on
the market stalls so that customers
can make their choice (below).

"Da coc mà boc trung gà ; bô ra thom
ngat, ca nhà muon an. Là cai gi ? - Là qua
mit'. (A riddle: the skin of a toad wrapped around
eggs; when opened the delightful odour makes
the whole household want to eat it.
The answer is - a jackfruit.)

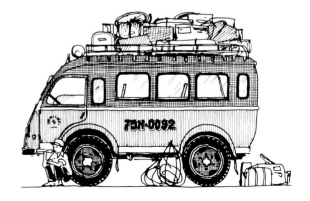

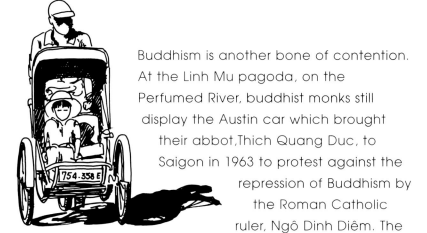

Buddhism is another bone of contention. At the Linh Mu pagoda, on the Perfumed River, buddhist monks still display the Austin car which brought their abbot, Thich Quang Duc, to Saigon in 1963 to protest against the repression of Buddhism by the Roman Catholic ruler, Ngô Dinh Diêm. The abbot immolated himself. At the time, North Vietnam supported the spirit of sacrifice of the monks and their pacifism. Today, the monks of the Bao Quoc pagoda and other bastions of Buddhism are distancing themselves from the ' B.K. ' (*Bac Ky*, the Northerners), since the religious revival, which ironically is the result of their policy of tolerance, has not met with their unqualified approval.

Since the reunification, Hué seems to have rediscovered its natural place as a cultural centre, and by extension a tourist attraction. It is to be hoped that the usual unfortunate consequences - haphazard building and vulgar commercialism - do not ensue.

In 1981, UNESCO decided to save Hué, 'an integral part of the indivisible heritage of humanity'. Since then it has been restored, rehabilitated and rebuilt, but much remains to be done. The city and its citadel will never recapture its lost delights, which have vanished forever, but there is a strong desire to recreate it by planning an esthetic layout and attempting to preserve a way of life that is so heavily threatened by

Western sub-cultures. As long ago as 1916, in a magazine produced by the Friends of Old Hué, the following words appeared: ' ...these pages devoted to picturesque Hué ...revive for them (the readers) the Hué which we now see but which will soon disappear'.

Today, although modernism - and especially the evils of concrete construction - has already done its work, Hué retains something of its discreet, modest and even haughty charm. Of course, this 'masterpiece of urban poetry', as Hué has been called, has had the colonial imprint grafted on to it. A few structures left over from the French administration have been taken over by the city. They include the bridge formerly called after Clémenceau, and some crumbling colonial-style villas with their balconies, balustrades and stuccoed facades. There is also the ponderous and vainglorious 'Catholic folly', the Church of the Redeemer of Vinh Loi. The best way

Hué is a city in the country where one can pick lotuses on the river bank or cycle in the shady streets, which are more like country lanes (opposite). It is not unusual to see fishermen throwing their nets into the river running through it (right).

to see the real modern Hué is to cycle to the street-markets of An Cuu or Bên Ngu or to cross the Tràng Tiên and Phu Xuân bridges, and take Trân Hung Dao Avenue to the Dông Ba market, the 'belly of Hué'. Join the throng of cyclists, barges, the old ladies in their ao dài (tunics) and the market gardeners who make good-humoured remarks about the foreign tourists. In the evening, one can linger among the bookstalls on Lê Loi Avenue, where English grammars and computer books are sold along with heavily-thumbed editions of *Kim Van Kiêu*, an 18th-century classic, alongside American paperbacks. If one tires of this 'feast for the eyes', one can always resort to a waterside restaurant and feast upon more material delicacies which are hard to describe but not to remember. There are *banh bôt loc* (manioc paste

The modern buildings of Hué are an attractive mixture of little shops, colonial residences, the town houses of the scholars of old and narrow streets of brightly-painted modest dwellings. Opposite, it is siesta time on a street in the eastern district, and only the bicycles remain in the sun.
A handsome colonnaded mansion with painted shutters, is evidence of the former colonial presence (upper right-hand photo). Inside a mansion, the altar to the ancestors, on the left, is marked by characters on lacquered wooden panels and a buddhist image (below).

65

© Cornu

dumplings), *nem Hué* (fermented pork pâté), vermicelli with beef, stewed lotus seeds or mandarins from Huong Can. With luck, one can make the acquaintance of students from the Universities of Su Pham or Tong Hop, only too happy to practise their English. Wandering around a strange city, making unscheduled stops and having chance meetings are what endears a city and its life to the casual visitor. Of course, life is not always a bowl of cherries in Hué. Even though many of its inhabitants are nostalgic for its lost glories, all are happy that peace has been restored, though many are apprehensive about the future. Hué has experienced so much damage in the past, it looks to the future as a challenge.

Hué's future may well lie in its glorious past. The gold and ivory and the brocaded concubines of the Palace have vanished. The 'Lament for a Lost Capital City' chanted by blind musicians is no longer heard. The love songs of the sampan-dwellers on the River of Perfumes are no longer heard. They have vanished, along with the underglaze blue porcelain of which the orientalist, Father Cadière, wrote in 1915: 'What a shame that in order to find the most beautiful blues of Hué, one has to seek them in France'. But this magnificent

*The lotus is eaten as a vegetable, its seeds
are made into confectionery, its leaves are
used to flavour rice, and its flowers scent tea
and are offered on buddhist altars
(previous pages).*

*Traditional crafts survive in Hué, such as
this maker of large boxes (trong chau)
used for festivals in the province of Thua
Thiên Hué (left-hand photo).
The citizens earn much of their income
from cultivating smallholdings on the
ramparts of the Citadel
(left-hand photo above).
Ancient chores also survive, such as the
hand-washing of laundry (opposite).*

past is all part of the story of Hué and its place in history. Clearly, modernism, foreign influence and the social and economic changes will have their effect. Yet it is to be hoped that it will be able to absorb them, manage them and dilute them without letting them change it for the worse. Hué must be allowed to build its future while having the will and the resources to preserve its past.

In the words of a local song, 'Wherever I go, I miss Hué...' But if the deep attachment which the people of Hué feel for their native or adopted city is to persist, Hué needs to retain its classical tradition as a seat of learning, a keen sense of its nuances, its aristocratic but pleasant air of distinction and above all, the authenticity of its customs and way of life, including the elegant women in traditional dress and the activity along the River of Perfumes.

Discussion can become heated in the Cho Dông Ba, *the city's fruit and vegetable market (above).*
The bridges have also played their part in the life of Hué. The gentle wooden arch of the Thanh Toan bridge, dates from the 19th century;
it has recently been restored and is one of the beauty spots on the outskirts of the city (left-hand page, above). The iron Tràn Tiên bridge
(formerly the Clémenceau bridge) is crowded from early morning with hordes of cyclists and rickshaws (centre). The railway bridge (Câu
Da Viên) crosses the river and the train runs parallel to the ditches around the Citadel (below, left).

HUÉ IN DEPTH

It was no exaggeration. The travellers of old, the emperor-poets and the writers of colonial times were all telling the truth. More recently , so were the journalists and the authors of the tourist guides. All of them said and wrote that Hué was surrounded by a particular aura and had an attraction which no painter, no writer and no photographer was ever quite able to capture. Could it be because Hué exercises a magical attraction, a sort of spell?

The countryside around Hué is part of this attraction and of the harmony of the site chosen for the capital by the last imperial dynasty, that of the Nguyên. Everywhere, vegetation harmonises with the stones and stonework. The shores of the

River of Perfumes are lively yet peaceful. The river winds lazily down to the South China Sea. The grandeur of the remains of the Citadel mingles with the tragic air of melancholy emanating from the last resting-places of the rulers, which merge into the surrounding vegetation. At dusk, in perfect harmony with the sights and sounds that enriched the day, the delicacies of the local cuisine tempt the palate. As a counterpoint, the slim, graceful silhouettes of the young women of Hué can be seen moving sinuously in their traditional silken tunics in shades of purple. Once the initial feelings of strangeness and surprise have passed, they are replaced by an unexpected enthusiasm. The body is enveloped in the moist tropical heat. There are constant showers whose droplets soak and trickle. In the autumn, these showers become torrents, bringing the city to a

The Mountain of the King's Screen forms a natural protective barrier against the ill winds of Sino-Vietnamese geomancy (left). A bronze lion from the mausoleum of Thieu Tri emits a silent roar (right).

'On a beautiful winter's night it is not cold; not a ripple on the River of Perfumes. The wind can hardly be felt, the rowing-boat does not move'.
(Poem by the emperor Tu Duc).

standstill, stopping the traffic and causing unexpected floods. Exoticism is the norm, whether it is in the ingenuity of the craftsmen or the liveliness of the street vendors, but it can also be misleading. The sweetness of the air does not exclude the rigours of life. One may be influenced by an ancient poem or story which leads to flights of the imagination. The image of the ancient capital may have been magnified in ones' mind until it has taken on gigantic proportions. This imperial city may have been endowed with a majesty, a magnificence which exists only in Peking, on which it was modelled. Beneath the outwardly pleasant way of life, Hué conceals a provincial lassitude which gives it its outdated and melancholy air. It is hard to decide whether it is the decline and impoverishment of the city which gives it the langorous appeal of a bygone era, or whether it is the aging attractions of the ancient ramparts, the princely palaces and the haunting mausoleums.

Hué may seem to be preoccupied with its past. The still waters of the

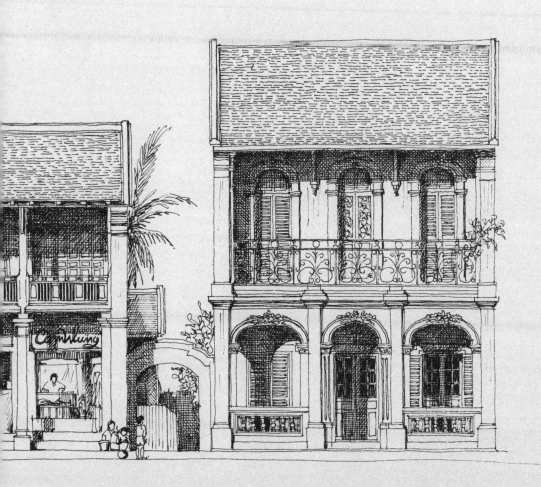

many lakes, the dilapidated palaces abandoned to weeds and mosses and the tombs of long-dead emperors are constant reminders of its tortured history.

Yet the city of today is experiencing a constant process of change. It has its own special culture and is suffused with a new energy which it is striving to manage.

In trying to discover the essence of Hué, should one discreetly slide open its doors, slip inside its rooms and fumble about, on the stage and in the wings, seeking to distinguish between the real and artificial, the present and the past.

An imaginary street in Hué showing French colonial houses, shops, and traditional homes. (facing).

Geomancy and Water Courses

"A masterpiece of urban poetry" is how Amadou-Mabtar M'Bow, General Director of UNESCO described Hué in 1981, when he launched the international campaign for the protection of the site. This allegory of harmony between man and the cosmos, also represents a remarkable example of technical achievement and the optimum use of the land within the physical limitations of the site.

Two key writings need to be referred to in order to fully comprehend the site:
- the first is symbolic, inspired by Chinese geomancy (*feng shui*) based on the golden rule of the Book of Changes (the Kinh Dich, written in 550 B.C.).
- the other is pragmatic, based on ancient knowledge of the waters. These are the salt waters of the China Sea, so menacing when a typhoon threatens, the fresh waters of the River of Perfumes with its predictable floods and the sudden, torrential rains (more than 3000 mm of precipitation in less than three months).

This poetic dialogue is based on the constant quest for a subtle balance between submission to the natural order and a proud desire to master it. In this respect, Hué constitutes a genuine imperial challenge to the natural order of the elements and the permanence of water.

A geomantic interpretation of the site

Lê Quy Don, a practitioner of geomancy, adviser to the emperor Nguyen Phuc Khoat (1738 - 1765) and planner of the palace and its surrounding city, wrote:

'When sitting and looking south-east, being supported by the earth's spinal column, facing the row of kneeling hills, a great river in the foreground, the area is as big as one's hand, the water enters on the right and the place is rich in power, the dragon bows and the tiger sits, a beautiful position desired by heaven, this site deserves to be the capital of kings'.

According to the rule, a site conveys as much vital power as the favourable conjunction of cosmic energies allows. The wind carried in the veins of the Dragon (mountainous peaks) is tempered or amplified by flowing waters, especially by a river whose entrance to the site (the Dragon's Head) must be visible and situated on the right when looked at by humans.

Thus Hué's main cosmic force is drawn from the north from the hill of Triều Sơn Đông of which the Huyen Yen bridge constitutes the head, from the South-East from the hill of Nui Ngu Binh, the gate protecting the inner City and the two islets situated on either side of the Citadel in the East, personifying the beneficent breath of the Azure Dragon and in the west, the pernicious breath of the White Tiger. The River of Perfumes enters on the right in relation to the Citadel. This deep rift separates the Imperial City on the East bank, that of the rising sun, from the Valley of the Tombs on the West Bank and that of the setting sun.

Perfect control over the natural surroundings

Behind this magical incantation lies a clever usage of the natural topography.

In choosing this elbow-bend in the River of Perfumes, the emperor Gia Long realised that he could use this water course to supply the City with plenty of fresh water and discharge the dirty water which collected naturally into a natural depression situated downstream of the Citadel. The channelling of two branches of the river, known as Kim Long

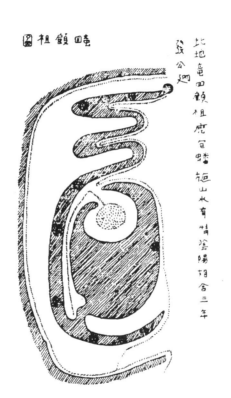

and Bach Yen supplied the Royal Canal (Ngu Ha) with water as well as the two defensive ditches of the moat. A judicious system of gutters, channels and reservoirs to capture rainwater made it possible to maintain virtually the same water level both inside and outside the three city walls, thus protecting the Citadel from flooding until 1945.

Failure to maintain the canals, the deterioration of the network of underwater channels and the gradual overfilling of the lakes have endangered this entire system of man-made water-ways. Water has again conquered the site, accelerating the slow deterioration of the imperial buildings which had managed to survive the horrors of the bombing. The restoration of this water control system, which is now under way, is one of the most important initiatives of the architectural and landscape site, which is listed in the World Heritage register.

Art in Hué

The art of Hué is largely decorative and ornamental. Annamese artists concentrated mainly on producing stylised versions of natural forms, animal, vegetable and mineral. Although they have not restricted themselves to representations of nature, their work is imbued with specific and profound meaning, and they have always adhered to traditional standards and codes.

Annamese art is based on the fluidity and complexity of shapes, repeated patterns and transformations.

Is there anything distinctive about Annamese art? There is, indeed, an art which is unique to central Vietnam, and which has been influenced by the imperial dynasties. Some of its features are delicate sculptures, narrow beams, lacework patterns in wood and graceful lines.

Most of the ornamental elements are of 19th century origin, but a few date from the 18th century. These include:

Geometric patterns

Ornamental geometric patterns are often used as backgrounds or the basis for decoration. The three main motifs used are the lattice, the circle and the fret.

The lattice may be diamond-shaped, reticulated, hexagonal, tortoiseshell or triangular. The circle is often used in the representation of a gold coin (several concentric circles) or shown as two interlocking or interlinked circles (having a religious significance). It may also be transformed into a rhomboid or oval.

Fretting is the most frequently encountered pattern, which in Chinese and Annamese symbology represents "the line that returns" upon itself, folds in upon itself and is extended. The most common fretwork patterns are cruciform and swirling. These are used for framing, for decorating a corner or the tip of a beam, roof rafters or the handle of a vase. Fretwork can even be an item of furniture in its own right, such as a shelf, and it is often decorated with an inanimate object or a plant.

Chinese Characters

Ideograms were used to represent an object, an activity or an idea. They are eminently decorative. Modern Chinese characters are more remote from the original ideograms but retain their ornamentation. Thus the use of such characters as happiness (phúc), longevity (tho) or joy (hi). They are often extremely stylised, being reduced to their simplest form and shown as a few curving or angular lines, or sometimes even a simple rectangle.

Inanimate objects

Many inanimate objects are used in Annamese ornamentation. These are mainly cult objects, such as incense-burners, incense vases and containers to hold joss-sticks and candelabra. The scroll rolled up at both ends to form a cartouche is used mainly for panels inscribed with mottos. The burning globe appears normally in the centre of the roof ridge of pagodas. The calabash is used less frequently, as are acorns and fringes. A series of eight so-called precious objects, including a fan, a flute and a paintbrush-holder are used on frameworks and partitions.

Leaves, flowers and fruits

The vegetable kingdom is represented by foliage, flowers, plants and fruit. It is sometimes hard to identify the leaves and flowers since they are so heavily stylised by the artist. However, the leaves of ficus, peach and plum blossom, the water-lily, bamboo and peony are often the inspiration. Fruits include the pear, the peach, the form of the citron known as the hand of Buddha and the sweetsop or anona.

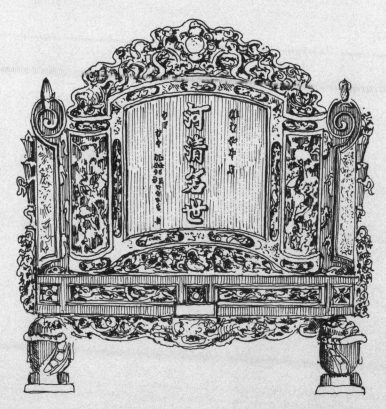

The symbolism attached to each item adds to the charm of the ornamentation. For example, the pomegranate is a symbol of fertility, pine and bamboo symbolise immortality and the peach represents a young girl.

Animals

Four animals reputed to have supernatural powers occupy pride of place in the Annamese bestiary. These are the dragon, the unicorn, the phoenix and the tortoise. They also have a religious significance and their representation is a sign of mystic influence. Through their imagery, they communicate the qualities they possess or which they symbolise. This is also true of the less-important animals such as the crane, the lion, the bat and the fish.

When the dragon is used to symbolise the emperor, its feet have five claws. Elsewhere, they only have four. The dragon is used in general to represent man, the husband or the betrothed, whereas the phoenix represents the wife and feminity. The dragon is a popular symbol in Hué and is to be found on roofbeams, staircases, embroidery, painted panels - in other words, everywhere.

The unicorn, that mythical and fabulous beast, is the symbol of kindness and its horn is a sign of peace. "The hoofprints of the unicorn" designates the imperial line. It is used to pattern pagoda screens and as general decoration. The tortoise is a symbol of eternity and is thus often forms a support or bracket for a plaque.

From 'The Art of Hué', New edition
Association des Amis du Vieux Hué

The consoles and overhanging eves of the roofs are cleverly designed and adorned with elegant carvings (photo, top). A handsomely decorated imperial screen (above).

Annamese Ceremonies

On the occasion of its elaborate and colourful ceremonies, the palace of Hué was roused from the lethargy into which the austere and stultified protocol, based on that of the Imperial court of Peking, caused it to sink.

These included the Festival of Têt, in honour of the Vietnamese New Year, during which services were held in the imperial pagodas and temples. This was also when the mandarins renewed their oath of allegiance to the 'Emperor, by coming to prostrate themselves before his throne.

On the occasion of the Spring Walk, the emperor, carried in a chair and escorted by the princes of the royal blood as well as by civilian and military mandarins, was paraded around the city 'for the pleasure of his subjects', as it states in the regulations. By presenting himself alternately on the two banks of the River of Perfumes, the Emperor invoked all the divine benedictions.

Another ceremony took place every three years on the Mount of Heaven (Nam Giao) south of Hué. This time, seated in a chariot drawn by an elephant and surrounded by two thousand soldiers, the Annamese emperor came to pay homage to the Earth and the Heavens in the presence of his whole court. After performing ritual acts and dances of purification, wine was distributed in honour of the Heavens and the Earth, while a young buffalo was burned to appease the spirits. The Emperor officiated in person by prostrating himself and offering jade, incense, food and wine to the Heavens

Court ceremonial even fascinates the modern visitor. Here, tourists from Hanoi pose in the costume of a mandarin.

82

and the Earth. Each of these gestures was part of an extremely complex religious ritual which the sovereign had to follow to the letter or the entire country might have had to suffer the consequences of divine displeasure.

Of all the ceremonies, one of the most important was the coronation of a new emperor. Numerous contemporary accounts give an accurate impression of the last such investiture held at the imperial palace on 8 January, 1926. On that date, which was chosen by the court astrologers, the Forbidden City of Hué was gripped with feverish agitation. From early morning, courtiers, followed by the many eunuchs who lived in the Palace, dashed about making the final preparations for the time-honoured and unchanging ceremony. The Ngo-mon Gate, which had remained closed since the death of the previous monarch, was symbolically re-opened on this festive occasion to allow the official procession to enter, preceded by a squadron of lancers dressed in red. Wherever one looked, there was an array of magnificent costumes, brilliant silks, lacquered podiums and symbolic banners. Prince Vinh-Thuy, aged only 12, marched into the magnificent Palace of Supreme Harmony, wearing a yellow robe, his head covered in a cap encrusted with precious stones. He became the Emperor Bao-Daï, meaning 'Greatness rediscovered', the moment the name of his reign had been written in the Golden Book, and he had taken his seat on a throne decorated with dragons. The semi-darkness highlighted the golden glints of the costumes, and the new emperor, holding the symbolic sceptre, first received the salute and greetings from the Governor-General of Indochina then from the Senior Resident. The entire retinue, which apart from senior French officials consisted of princes of the blood, the Minister of Ritual and the Minister of War, were impressed by the gravity with which the monarch replied to the representatives of France before leaving in a palanquin for the great esplanade where the mandarins awaited him, in impeccable order. The civil mandarins were lined up in front of the Emperor. In the first row, stood the Third and Fourth Column of the Empire (the Minister of Justice and the Minister of the Interior) in their distinctive yellow tunics. Behind them stood the leading dignitaries, then the lesser functionaries. On the other side of the esplanade, were the military mandarins led by dignitaries with the rank of field-marshall, also robed in yellow silk. The style of dress, colour and insignia worn indicated the rank of nobility and function of each dignitary. On both sides of the road, the court heralds proclaimed the ritual commands which punctuated the ceremony. 'Kneel! Prostrate yourselves! and adore! Stand up!' and rhythmically, the mandarins prostrated themselves 19 times while a great dignitary chanted a long liturgy while kneeling. At that moment, the new Emperor truly became Le Duc Hoang Dí, the supreme judge who incarnates the Law and who is above all 'the father and mother of his people'.

84

Heritage and Modernity

The Imperial City and the Valley of the Tombs in the process of restoration

Since the first campaign was launched to save the city and rural surrounding of Hué, in 1981, the Vietnamese authorities have become aware of the economic and cultural asset of this valuable heritage. First a Centre for the Conservation of Historic Monuments was created, then an area including the Citadel and the Valley of the Tombs was declared protected in 1991. At the same time, the site was included in the list of World Heritage Sites in 1993.

Donations by governments and private philanthropists from all over the world helped the Vietnamese government and the local authorities of the Province of Hué in the rehabilitation of a site which had been badly damaged by thirty years of war and a merciless climate. The Palace of Supreme Harmony (Dien Thai Hoa) and the South Gate (Ngo Mon) of the Imperial City were restored to their former glory. It is once again possible to admire the magnificent and precise geometry of the Mausoleum of Minh Mang or to lose oneself in the baroque curlicues of the Tomb of Khai Dinh. Progressively, The city is reorganising the magnificent landscaping and architectural project to recreate the glories of the last imperial dynasty. More than 170,000 foreign visitors came in 1995 to admire the harmony and experience the serenity of this, the 'pearl of Asia'.

A much greater heritage than the imperial tradition

The imperial legacy of the Citadel and the Valley of the Tombs are only part of the legacy of Hué's historic buildings. Once the city became the permanent home of the court in 1802, a Chinese city began to develop north-east of the Citadel. The first trading posts date from the 17th century, and some still stand in the ancient river port of Huong Vinh. To the South-west of the Citadel, at Kim Long, one can still see the vestiges of the country houses of the scholars who came to write or to listen to poetry, soothed by the sweet air of the River of Perfumes. The French settled on the opposite bank, south of the Citadel, in 1875. The emperor ordered a screen of tall trees which would allow him to look from earth to sky without having to see the building of the colonial city, criss-crossed by wide avenues, with its administrative buildings and delightful villas in the Norman style. Le Havre was one of the main ports of embarcation for Indochina for the colonists, who came with their families and their plans for their future homes. The Cham heritage is omnipresent despite the almost total disappearance of their monuments. They live in the collective memory, in their venerated sites, the prayers to the spirits of the departed and the temples encountered at the corner of each narrow street.

The landscape heritage of Hué, the garden city

The essence of the city is to be found in the way it blends in with its surroundings. Geomancy governed the siting of the Citadel. All the imperial buildings obey the laws of *feng shui* in their orientation, layout and ornamentation, thus ensuring that they meet the requirements for the man-god to be in harmony with the cosmos.

This poetic dialogue between man and nature is one in which all the inhabitants of Hué are able to share. Each house in Hué is a microcosm, embodying the same geomantic rules in the orientation of the building, the arrangement of the garden and the water-courses.

The town that has grown up around the imperial city disappears in a maze of narrow, tree-lined streets, where behind a carefully tended hedge stand houses prudently shaded by palms. The village of Kim Long is a shining example of this harmony, born of a perfect adaptation of the dwelling to an environment in which the sun beats down mercilessly.

The threat of urban modernisation

Beyond the importance of preserving the heritage for posterity and for tourism, there is a vibrant, living city of 300,000 inhabitants which has naturally settled into the site. Between 1968 and 1980, many families from the country sought protection from the bombing behind the massive ramparts of the Citadel and built ramshackle dwellings which in the course of time were turned into permanent homes. Buildings which once housed imperial ministries and the larger colonial villas have been turned into public buildings. The whole of the university of Hué which has an annual intake of 12,000 students is built inside the Citadel or the former colonial city. the university districts are the most central and best served by infrastructure and transport networks. They are favoured sites for densification and urban modernisation.

When Vietnam opened its doors to the market economy in 1989, the appetites of local and international investors were whetted. This new impetus has been translated into intensive and rapid construction, often uncontrolled. Old buildings were converted haphazardly, roads encroached upon, services and infrastructure reached saturation point and lakes and gardens began to disappear. The urgency of the rebuilding of the economy and the demographic pressures explain the speed of this development which the financial resources of the city could not control. This spontaneous modernisation has threatened to distort the original town plan and the balance between landscape and architecture at this historic beauty spot.

The threat of tasteless restoration

The Vietnamese authorities have expressed the desire to rehabilitate the imperial decor and in the long term, restore all of the palaces and temples of the imperial city. Hué would play an important economic role. It would become a lasting tourist attraction, involving the progressive modernisation of the local rice-growing economy which is particularly impoverished.

This reconstruction project would seem to be all the more natural since the Asian world does not have

the same concept of heritage as does the West. Unlike Europe which is deeply attached to the preservation of the forms and organisation of historic buildings, in Asia the symbolic reading of an inscription on an edifice in a rural landscape is considered sufficient. The prestige of a monument rests more in the value of the site and the view it offers than the buildings erected on it. Furthermore, the identical reconstruction using modern materials is often considered to be more respectful of the spirit of the building than a long and unsatisfactory genuine restoration.

There is a danger of erecting pastiches aimed at gullible tourists and of eradicating any trace of authenticity. To what extent should the imperial city, more than 70 per cent of which was destroyed by the War, be rebuilt? Should it be reconstructed in its entirety? The palaces and temples destroyed in the bombings have left a huge wasteland in their wake. The strangeness of this space is charged with a nostalgia as great as that which emanates from those monuments which survived.

Should the whole economy of the city be disrupted in order to transform the heart of Hué into a sort of international tourist museum? There are 70,000 people living in the Citadel, which was originally built to house 10,000. The implementation of a heritage restoration project requires resources which a town in a developing country would find it hard to muster.

The modern city built over the ruins of the ancient one cannot be ignored. The charm of Hué is also and above all its inhabitants. A successful reconstruction to attract tourists would depend both on the quality of the restoration work and on the re-creation of an authentic environment.

Defining a new harmony between buildings and the landscape

The restoration of historic Hué involves defining a town-planning policy which would involve preserving the heritage without denying modern urban dynamics. The Vietnamese authorities are doing their best. A master plan has been devised which places manufacturing operations outside the city walls, thus confining subordinate administrative and tourist operations to central Hué. The plan requires the drafting of regulations which would introduce a new urban harmony, a fair balance between the scale of hotel-building projects and other tourist facilities and the scale of the environment. Height and size restrictions on buildings must be accompanied by careful landscaping and the sensitive conversion to different uses of the renovated buildings, as well as a policy of consciousness-raising among the local citizenry.

All the local inhabitants must contribute to the restoration of Hué. The crafts used in the original construction of the buildings must be revived, as should the other arts which flourished in the city, such as Vietnamese literature and poetry. The future of Hué belongs more than ever to its inhabitants and their desire to reaffirm their cultural identity.

Published in 1997 by ASA EDITIONS. Capitals of Legend and Les Editions d'Indochine are registered trademark of ASA EDITIONS

Publishers: Thomas Renaut & Marc Wiltz; Series design: Thomas Renaut and Roland Neveu; Picture Editor: Roland Neveu; Layout and photographs: Thomas Renaut ; Additional photography: Jean Luc Cornu (p68h), Ecole Française d'Extrême Orient (p8, p9, p14b), Fonds Grafeuil (p10, p11, p12, p14h, p15), Francis Engelmann Collection, (p6, p7, p13) Illustrations: Jean Christophe Marchal and François Grek ; Text and captions by Michel Hoang; Additional text by Thierry Deslot (Annamese Ceremonies) and Myriam Laidet (Geomancy, Heritage and Modernity), Colour separations: Rainbow (Hong Kong); Printing: Paramount (Hong Kong); Film Laboratories: Supervision, Bangkok. English translation: Josephine Bacon, Chanterelle Translations.

For information about the series, contact ASA Editions, PARIS (Tel: +33-1-42 27 75 00 Fax: +33-1-42 27 75 05)

Acknowledgements: Catherine Faudemay and Hervé Jevardat, Marie Sybille de Vienne, Jacques Népote, Jean Pierre Ducrest, Françoise Chappuis, Rémi Boutinet and Charles Nitot, Henri Charles Blanc, Frédéric Durand, Jean Claude and Colette Bernay, Jean Pierre Vandenhende, Mme Do Thi Phan, Dominique Natot, Cati Forget and Jean Philippe Poulain, Minja Yang and Réjanne Hervé.
Thanks also to all the team of Esprit Direct and specially Jean-Philippe Vaisse
Very special thanks for their support throughout this project is due to Geneviève Piot-Coliche, Sabrina Schliwanski, Anne Waxin and Jean-Luc Cornu.

ISBN : 2-911589-13-0

By choosing to devote 1% of its regional budget on international cooperation, the Nord-Pas de Calais region of France has consciously chosen solidarity and the quest for a fairer balance between the so-called wealthier countries and the developing countries. The relative comfort in which even the poorest of us live cannot be compared to the situation of those peoples who are unable currently to satisfy their most basic needs, those of health, education, and self-sufficiency in food. The Saint Louis region of Senegal, Kayes in the French Mali, the southern regions of Poland and the Moghilev region of Belarus are already part of the scheme. The provinces of central Vietnam are a long way from Hanoi and Ho Chi Minh City, places which are much sought after and considered desirable, and we wanted to work with this remote region in order to create a partnership and initiate mutual development.

In 1993, we chose the provinces of Quang Nam Danang and Thua Tien Hué, whose long-term development will guarantee greater national cohesion between north and south Vietnam.
We have been cooperating in many projects, among them:

- recycling of waste water using natural reservoirs in Danang, with recovery of waste,
- organising waste collection in Hué,
- setting up a friendly society for the poorest peasants,
- creation and improvement of dispensaries.
- exchanges of technical personnel and aid in defining a strategic development plan,
- support for the study and propagation of the French language.

All of these projects are being run with input and close collaboration from Vietnamese citizens and technicians under a political, decentralised cooperation agreement, between town and town, citizen and citizen.

We chose to sponsor and give financial support to this book about Hué because we were convinced that this 'provincial city' deserved better than being merely listed as a one- or two-day excursion in the guided tour brochure.
The tombs, the Citadel and the Imperial City, which are the most often mentioned, ought not to be allowed to obscure the amazing conjunction between the architectural heritage and the ingenuity by which the surprising harmony is achieved between the natural environment, the architectural heritage and the human inhabitants; this is what lies behind the originality, the rhythm and the very soul of this city. In a fragile but exciting balance, houses, gardens, verdant ramparts, pools and natural lagoons give meaning and life to the local development of the surrounding area which has become part of the city.
Any overblown town-planning scheme or one which would involve complex technologies which the inhabitants would be incapable of mastering due to their level of solvency would irremediably upset those few towns which have escaped the high-productivity models which are suffocating us. Hué constitutes an example and a challenge for creating a new concept of modernity, which we are classifying by using the term 'sustainable development'.

The Vietnamese people have long lived through foreign domination, war and thus the urgency of survival. Today, in a land which is open and at peace, we hope that it will be possible to plan and create urban and rural landscapes supported by a harmonious balance between ancient traditions based on wisdom, respect for all life forms, solidarity and the legitimate desire of the population to gain access to moderate wealth which is shared equitably and guaranteed for all.

    Preserving and enhancing the existing at the service of the well-being of the populations is our ultimate aim.

RÉGION
NORD
PAS DE CALAIS

CONSEIL RÉGIONAL

MARIE-CHRISTINE BLANDIN
Chair of the Regional Council
Nord-Pas de Calais

The Région Nord - Pas de Calais has had a permanent delegation since January, 1997, at 12 Han Thuyen Street, Hué